Praise for
HELD

"HELD is a collection of cosmic connections, the deep grounding roots of grief, and the blooms that unfurl through the work of healing in community and in communion with nature. Lorenz Mazon Dumuk's debut collection celebrates the way our spirits are held by the natural beauty and inherent joy of this planet, as well as the stories we carry for our ancestors—stories that sometimes act as instructions for spiritual survival. In this collection, asteroids become collisions to reckon with in the body, and men learn to dismantle the 'disconnection between heart and mind' in order to 'love the singularity of one's self.' Dumuk writes for all of us who sometimes feel we are not enough—and reminds us that we are trees and peacocks waiting to discover our own celestial sexiness, a 'spell of loving the self' that spans across lifetimes and otherworldly portals of existence."
—**SUZY QUEZADA**, Educator/Poet

"Lorenz Mazon Dumuk is a poet of great compassion, generosity, and humor—and his debut book of poetry, HELD, celebrates all of those attributes of self. Whether he is communing with his ancestors and family, examining the many facets of himself, or exploring the idea of manatee farts, Dumuk brings a deep resonance of heart and soul into every poem. In his poem, 'Offspring of Victor Frankenstein,' he writes, 'at least a name would help bind / the collection that is you.' In the same way, these poems are naming, breath, laughter, and prayer bringing the pieces of the poet and his words together into a beautiful, lyrical wholeness."
—**ANDREA BLYTHE**, author of *Twelve: Poems Inspired by the Brothers Grimm Fairytale*

"The function of the poet, the storyteller, is not to be wise but to say what needs to be said memorably. The poems of Lorenz Mazon Dumuk are seeds that blossom into trees of memory, pain, love, heart, and all that is human. Al Robles once said the best part of our struggle is our poetry. I concur; the poems of Lorenz Dumuk show that our struggle can be shaped into beauty. His poems are seeds of wisdom that he shares, seeds that speak words we are afraid or ashamed to speak but grow from courage and bloom into wisdom that only the poet can speak."
—**TONY ROBLES**, "The People's Poet," author of *Where the Warehouse Things Are*

"This debut collection brings readers together as community, encircling us with the feeling of being HELD and home. Lorenz Mazon Dumuk spreads his feelings across each page, urging readers to 'return to the garden within.' HELD breathes life into the past by reuniting us with familial memories, while nurturing the future through visions of self and communal love. In the poem 'I Enter Eden,' Dumuk writes, 'Seeds I have sown from joy…are blooming / beneath my feet as I walk.' HELD encourages us to take a step into the living world to see not only the beauty around us, but to listen to the whispers of our ancestors."
—**KELLY RITTER**, Editor, Sampaguita Press

"What happens to the body, to the soul, and to the self during rapturous moments? In reflection, in mourning? In joy? Lorenz Mazon Dumuk's debut full-length collection, HELD, is an exploration of just that—it observes the body in nature, among spirit, the spirit within the body. How these layers of have the ability to fold into, or upend, each other. Carrying a deep and serious love for community and family is not without its silliness. In one moment, we hold each other in our sadness and in the next, we're giggling about poop. HELD is about being human, returning and embodying one's self, fully, and what it means to hold each other."
—**KEANA AGUILA LABRA**, author of *The Language of Unbreaking*

HELD

POEMS

Lorenz Mazon Dumuk

Sampaguita Press

Copyright © 2024 by Lorenz Mazon Dumuk

Held
Published by Sampaguita Press
Sampaguita Press LLC
P.O. Box 731305
San Jose, CA 95173

www.SampaguitaPress.com

All rights reserved.

For information about permission to reproduce selections from this book, please contact SampaguitaPress@gmail.com.

Book design by Sampaguita Press
Cover artwork by Lorenz Mazon Dumuk

ISBN: 978-1-965439-02-9 (paperback)
ISBN: 978-1-965439-03-6 (ebook)

Dedicated to my mother,
Zenaida Mazon Dumuk
and my brother
Isidoro Mazon Dumuk,
for loving me before ever needing a reason to.
I have always felt held because of you two.

Contents

11	On the Days
12	My cousin Dawn dreamt
13	Moonlight
15	Vanga
17	shrink wrapped light
18	masculinity so tender,
20	Once and Always a Tree
21	Offspring of Victor Frankenstein
23	Gurfa
24	Rewire
25	how to hold my heart
26	Bow
28	mummified bees
29	Lineage
30	Idle
31	Viewfinder
32	Year I Became
35	Petals Against My Forehead
36	I Enter Eden
38	stagnant
39	Peace Be With Me
41	gift of self
43	Hatch
44	pi ces
45	Static
47	Portal
49	Ugly Heart
50	sapwood
51	Inheritance
55	as we long
56	commune with salt and water
57	cemented dream

58	excavated exclamation
59	Sexy Be
61	Flourish
62	Scaled Lifetime
63	ashes
64	To Heal
65	optic
66	I've been staring at battlegrounds within me,
67	How To Seduce a Tornado
68	when you were caterpillar
69	Whale Poop
70	Recollection of None
71	body of water
72	Thrive
74	tonight I am a galaxy of stars
75	Extinguish
76	ingress
77	apricity
78	when asked what my favorite color is
79	In a dark room I am eating
80	pillow our faces against
81	Held
83	implosion
84	I once was only thought,
85	Dear Sadness,
86	Notes & Acknowledgements

HELD

On the Days

on the days i feel i am not enough
i will bee my hand into the comb
hidden inside my chest
my fingers dripping with honey
i am rich with sweetness

on the days i feel i am not enough
i will peacock the wrinkles of my mind
stretch out my feathers and take up space
dance with pearlescent plumage
i am full of imagination

on the days i feel i am not enough
i will elephant out my lungs
shout the lost memories and heaviness
inhale the breath of today
i am filled with life

on the days i feel i am not enough
i will merman into the waves of my spirit
dive in even when i am aching
for the comfort of surface yet i push forward
i am an abundance of brave

on the days i feel i am not enough
i will stare into the mirror
let the silence of my face speak
until i am no longer covered in lies
i am enough

My cousin Dawn dreamt

about a party on a boat, invited
all the cousins without hesitation.
Presh was there, before we all could cry she
cracked open freshly baked bread
whose steam dried our eyes
before a tear had chance to shed.
We celebrated, because that is how we love.
We hear Jojo playing uke and he shook
his head when our faces got watery,
wanted us to join in song than sob,
so loudly we all sang. We danced
because day will come and we
must make most of this party.
We brought lumpia, pancit,
sinigang, empanadas, flan and all
foods we love. We shared with one
another and laughed as we told
stories over this meal. This boat
sailed us to a place our hearts
have been longing to go: to the cousins
and family we missed. We felt a bit
lost and broken since their physical
departure, but in this dream we have it all
even if only for a night. My cousin
Dawn dreamt us all to this boat,
how love made this voyage sweet.
I hope we all continue to dream
parties with each other, I
hope love never finds reasons to end
having parties with one other.

Moonlight

When that asteroid
hit my face I kept
telling the universe I was fine.
I remember watching pieces of myself
scatter away from me. I felt
craters where parts of me once were.
Always felt all were looking at me.
Examining and try to recall
what is absent since the collision,
what is missing from the wholeness I once was.
I begged the sun to quit
traveling my way or to try to bypass
me in their travel. But their hands
continued to touch my cheeks,
fingers grace light against my surface.
What torture to be loved
when all you want is to be forgotten.
I hid from the earth
but that gravitational pull
continues to pull me
even when I try to orbit somewhere else.
I muted everything at one point,
tuned all the voices, closed my eyes
and let the inside of me become dark.
Rotated in my own self loathing.
I wanted ugly to be my only truth.
Wanted a veil, wanted to disappear from it all.
Then I clumsily listened and heard
faint whispers directed towards me.
Poets speaking of me in admiration and awe.
Singers serenading to others
even in my weary glow. Lovers
dancing and embracing while claiming
I put them under a spell.
A child looked at me with wonder,

told me how they no longer felt
alone knowing my presence kept them company.
I let go and felt full,
felt whole in my own orb.
Release these feelings of incomplete,
and embrace who I am,
and surrender to be part of this
universe that had never stopped
making me a part of them.

Vanga

My Mother tells me the vanga I'm cleaning
is older than me, how my Nanay, my mother's Nanang,
used to make bagoong in those vases,
that they came from the house my Mom grew up in.
I asked my Mom to tell me more as I run my fingers
across the heavy ceramic,
coming to realization that my Nanay once
touched and used these regularly at one time.
Mom entertains my curiosity,
lightly smiles because she knows I'm thirsty for stories,
I smile because she gets to talk about her Nanang.
"Your Nanay would go to Bauang Beach to get bulilit.
A small type of mackerel mostly used for bagoong.
There wasn't tricycles at the time
but there were kalesas, a horse carriage,
which sometimes she would take
with you Auntie's Mom.
They would buy the bulilit
from the local fishermen by the beach.
Sometimes they would clean the fish by the beach
with the sea water. Never with fresh water though.
I asked her one time why not fresh water,
which your Nanay tells me you got to clean with
salt water or else there will be worms.
After they were done buying and cleaning the bulilit
they would take them home.
Before your Nanay would put them in the vanga
she would mix it with asin,
or sometimes just put the bulilit in the vanga
by layers while adding sea salt.
After she was done she would put
a cheese cloth to cover it and place a rubber band
around the lip of the vanga to keep it in place.
That one you are cleaning, that one
could make 6 months worth of bagoong."

I get a bit sentimental with the vanga in my hand
which my Mom notices and gets a little choked up as well.
I never knew how much home were in those vangas,
how plain looking they were to me
when my Mom first brought them over from the Philippines.
I think of my Nanay, I think of my Mom,
how I mix their spirits with the asin of my words
hoping they will always be preserved in my vanga.

SHRINK WRAPPED LIGHT

eternal fluorescent light brings a comfort most inhabitants of dark know, yet the day still lingers. a weary sun unclothing their radiant self, gradient layers removed and bleed the sky with hues only the still can witness. feels as if one should recite a prayer, it occurs that this is the prayer, manifesting as that golden sphere sinks into earth, night slowly engulfs this ritual, becomes what the day cannot be. breath taken, the air changes, walk into the limbo of the 7-Eleven. dimensional traveler into the certainty and uncertainty of spaces.

MASCULINITY SO TENDER,

father kisses soft lips
onto newborn son.

masculinity so tender,
boy receives feathers of affirmations,
takes leaps where fathers
only knew borders and fences,
boy becomes a flight of imagination.

masculinity so tender,
young man of ocean
gathers his mountain of tribulations,
arms sway for millenniums
until mountain lulls into boulders,
until boulders cradle into rocks,
until rocks dream into sand.

masculinity so tender,
fire carried inside a man
knows he can warm and care,
yet monitors his rage
which had burned recklessly
forests into ashes of regrets.

masculinity so tender,
when isolated and inactive
can frost into a glacier,
statue himself frozen,
loses reasons to thaw
himself out of the stiff bleakness.

masculinity so tender,
when I met a man
with masculinity so fragile
I saw a hurt boy shelled

inside an egg of a man,
how his clenched fist of knuckles
wanted to destroy me
could not believe I existed
thought I was a virus to his way of living
needed me to be broken like him,
so I heard his anger
which lead me to his hurt
that spoke of an absent love,
I surrendered space for him
witness him give permission to himself
to heal, to learn, to know tenderness.

masculinity so tender,
awoke the femininity
that was never separate,
bridge together creating
potential rather than limitations,
dismantled the disconnection
between heart and mind,
grown to love the singularity
of one's self while acknowledging
my interconnection with the wholeness
Which I am always a part of,
to be nothing and everything
a synchronism of discorded harmony

Once and Always a Tree

I gave up trunk, roots, and leaves for you my loves. I surrender all these memories of you all so that I could return to you all in whatever form I could. My memories of you all may no longer be a clarity I can retrieve but my love for you all is a feeling that does transpire even if I no longer carry a form of familiarity. Annak, I cried when I became once again, maybe because I felt so disconnected and confused. I caught sight of some of you from the window and I felt a gravity to touch you all yet this body was immobile to do anything. I heard your songs, the rustling of all your leaves, exhaling all the springs and summer you have accumulated, let the wind pluck those beautiful brown blades off your branches. I was enthralled how tall you all stood annak, how deeply you held the earth between your roots, how gracefully you took up space. First time I crawled to you all I knew you all again. I ached. I had nothing to remember yet you reminded me to hold you all and I could not help but sprout a smile. Annak, I no longer speak your language yet you communicate a love that draws me to you always. I will hug you all until this body asks I be here for more than a past once lived. This flesh does not ask I leave you all, only that I expand and grow to a truth that reflects what it means to live in this life with a wholeness. I love you annak. My promise to this flesh can wait a little longer, so I celebrate you annak. You are all always my annak.

Offspring of Victor Frankenstein

"I ought to be thy Adam."
he does not though.
when you are all				pieces from once
								wholes,
at least a name would help bind
the collection that is			you.
instead you feel				stitches
from a god who only		wanted
the creation of you
but not the being of	you.

when he calls you				fiend,
he can only see his				reflection in you.
forgets you did not consent to this		living,
yet interjects		his will
that you shall be a reality.

when he labels	you			spectre,
how haunted a spirit he is.
you are merely a house of		a body
that echoes all the ghost			he carries.
						his	delusion that the birth of you
would bring peace to				his madness,
   is but an unjust logic of			his own ego.

when he sees you as			wretch,
only he would know so well.
   breaking patterns of				life cycle
because the cycle of his current life
		brings				no real joy.
how villainous of him,
to expect you to be more
when you are					merely a sum
of all he hates about	himself.

when you submit to the world's perspective
of being this hideous monster,
were you surprised to how   truly terrified
they became of you.
did this   isolation   they push on
you,
make you want to make them feel your   hurt?
breathless you made others.
  lifeless they truly made you feel.

Gurfa

I want to rest in your hands
and be called sacred.
Fill all the channels of lines,
read the story of your palms,
kiss the fingertips that hold me.
I am an open prayer
cupped in your pair of hamsas.
Bring lips to me and quench.
Drink until the heat subdues.
May the fear of thirst flow out
become what you consume,
call thyself pure, cleanse, holy.

Rewire

I attempted to recreate you.
Composing atoms and DNA from memory.
I do not know where to put the gummy
bears in this helix of you,
so I linked it with swing ropes
you once let go to feel flight beneath your body.
I gathered all these eggs that these dead
butterflies laid since your absence,
made your skull with tomato leaves,
caterpillars flesh out your cheeks,
forehead, and chin, cocoons of silk
unwind and dyed with nights you left wishes on.
Piled these slices of pizza until
they formed your spine, watch cheese
spread across moving at the speed of your
neurons that have always shocked
me with electric feels. I opened a mostly empty
jar of bagoon that held these laughters of you I collected.
Chant them into the bellow of this accordion
I used to make your belly. I touch the keys,
they become your skin beneath my fingers.
Ripped all these cassettes, VHS of movies you
swore stole your stories and emotions,
mixtapes that were clones of tracks that connected
you to lovers and homies, unspooled ribbons I
massaged until your muscles toned into flesh
that I onced remember holding. These hummingbirds
and wrens you flocked into my chest
I begged to migrate back to you. They do not.
I watch them get lost into the open air.
I quit remembering you. I exhaled.
Knew I was not an alchemist of you.
Flew a kiss to the sky hoping it find its way to you.
Decomposed what I tried so hard to preserve,
let the earth and soil do what they have always done.

HOW TO HOLD MY HEART

maysa: find galaxies in my eyes, share the cosmic wonder in yours, watch until thousands of stars have died and emerged.
dua: water this garden in my chest. plant seeds and till the earth. make friends with these earthworms until they tell you secrets of this soil in me.
tallo: rest your palm on mine. settle our breaths until our pulse feel similar. create a bridge of tenderness that leaves me wanting to migrate into this hope with you.
uppat: watch all the feathered creatures flock to your fingertip. witness fins, scales, and gills swim into the pool in your hands. feel all the feet, hooves, and toes inch their way to you.
lima: feel roots dig into your skin. feel sun kiss all the soft and callous parts of you. feel tickles from an abyss that still longs to play even in the depth of darkness. feel a heart taking your invitation, your care, your bravery and calling it all scared and wanted.
innem: inhale
pito: exhale
walo: be

BOW

I matadored myself from missing you
    taunted these desires for you
waved
   around this blanket
      I have wrestled sleep with
felt my muscles
         tensed as the earth
               beneath me shook
uncaged toro from my ribs
     horns angry I
          could not make us work
keen in puncturing
   me with all their might

everytime   I   dodged an attack
I shook off the cape of my
      disguise
dust of poems   filled the air
while the world threw me   roses

again I am charged
    am pierced this time
         and bleeding
  my fabricated shield
     soaked itself with my
        wounds
I stand tall to prolong this illusion of being unharmed
crowd believes   I am a hero
I remained in the ring

I stared at this bull
    nostrils
expanding and
    compressing with every breath
hooves digging into the dirt as
they prepared to lunge

frustrated being,
        majestic creature,
                      survivor
I avoided these feelings for too long
        felt myself
                impaled
struck directly by their horn
          I forgot the crowd was watching
      forgot I was suppose to win
forgot why I was fighting

I begged for forgiveness
confessed that I was too
        coward to take care of them
admitted I did not want to feel the hurt

I saw their face
pressed my nose against their own
before they returned back into my chest

"Toro! Toro! You have returned"

MUMMIFIED BEES

unlike humans, there is no need for royalty to preserve the body of the deceased. unlike humans, one does not need to make promises or arrangements with the living to assist with afterlife rituals. unlike humans, there will be no pyramid erected nor slaves oppressed to push one's agenda. unlike humans, nothing happens if one is not praised or even cursed.

not every bee wishes to be mummified. there is a reason though honey can be found in tombs. there is a reason honey does not quickly perish or decompose as many other sources of nourishments do after time. there is a reason for honey's sweetness, stickiness, slowness. honey the time traveler.

bee choosing to mummy theirself is not preparing for death but committing to their birth. saying I will be born anew when all is done. some are drawn to this early on, some in later days, most do not care.

step one, buzz no one. bees are busy as is.
step two, make sure the hive is not dependent on the gathering of your honey. work vigorously to ensure their well being is thriving.
step three, find your favorite flowers. sing your songs of sober. sing your songs why you adore them. forget they do not understand bee. dance and serenade your attraction.
step four, find a hole in a tree, ground or rock.
step five, gather fallen petals and place all around your hole. use nectar to help things adhere to the walls. step five, collect nectar and place in hole. fan the nectar everytime to remove as much water.
step six, sing songs to the flowers again. you may be drunk at this time if you wish. dance and serenade one last time.
step seven, crawl into cramp hole. line outside hole with beeswax.
step eight, eat all the honey. eat until you are all honey. until honey is all you.

LINEAGE

wonder when she prays if she knows
she has been the prayer of many?

how once upon a time love found
its way to two people
and in their devotion and care for each other,
wanted to expand what love
meant for them and had her,
felt prayer manifested into reality
the moment they held her.

when her little hands come together
can she feel all the hands of those
who could not hug her in this lifetime?
how they held her in their prayers
that she is loved with abundance,
that the world continues to give
      her reasons to smile,
that she is protected in all she does.

I hope she prays to make this world
better even if it seems hopeless,
hope she prays not forgetting she is loved
especially from those blessed to be her parents,
hope she prays and laughs
   at all that is unplanned
     dares braves herself to keep going,
prays and cries in joy
   when all that goes right
     and dances in celebration,
prays and breathes with a wholeness
    knowing she is never truly lost
      especially when love is present in her.

IDLE

manatees use farts to help
navigate themselves through the different
depths of water. beautiful buoyant
balloon balancing natural
gasses within to access the many
different levels around.

I have fart memories.
I am not manatee with them though,
I wish I was. I release
and sink myself without thought,
burying myself within these kelps,
wanting to just drown myself there.
or I hold on, afraid I will never
see the surface again if I do,
trying to ignore all these memories in me
because it hurts to acknowledge they are there.
I want to manatee better,
work with these farting memories
and maybe get to these moments of vegetation
ready to be eaten by me with delight.
hold on certain fart memories
long enough so that I have reason and capabilities
to not sulk myself into what feels abysmal.
how natural these memories of farts,
how sacred of an air to keep us
afloat, to be let go… enough to
help us reach the places
waiting for us to arrive.

Viewfinder

What aperture do I
need to capture her?
Is it even possible when I can barely dial
my shutter speed when I am around her?
Maybe all my images of her
are bokeh and I am allured
by these refractions of light around her.
This might be the clarity I want though.
Seeing these saturated and
unsaturated points in life
composed in an intentional way to articulate
what the eye sometimes misses,
   what the heart wishes more would remember.
When I tell her she is the subject
I wish to focus on,
what I mean is that I have an ISO sensitivity for her,
that I am fascinated at how the light
travels around her,
how light emanates out that smile of hers
  bursts throughout her laugh which I catch
myself eager to hear over and over again.
I want to use as many rolls this life will give me,
to see what I can develop with her.

Year I Became

1979 is the year I became the 3rd son of Isidoro and Zenaida Dumuk. Was their last try for a girl. There would be no one to put into dresses, well she did put my middle brother in a dress when he was a toddler to visualize what would've been, and even placed me in one as well when I could fit in the same dress. My mother gave up dreams of a girl and proudly embraced being a mother of 3 sons.

1986 is the year I became a giant carton of Minute-Maid orange juice. Learned to be my Mom's libation of creativity. Morph into a box hand stapled together by her hands. Metal teeth that held everything together, would puncture my chubby skin if given the chance. Costume pierced for fixes of blood, even took my Mom's hemoglobins as she fabricated through the weeks to bring this costume into fruition. Felt simultaneously trapped and beautiful when hermit into my new shell. Wore an orange sweater to give the illusion my visible arms, which stuck outside fabricated holes, were these freshly squeezed citrus people loved. Understood that time around the sun what it meant to be my Mother's pride; that her heart was a multitude of goodness outpouring in everything she did; armored myself as her son.

1989 I was a broken scale. Needle wanting to tip to the approval of my Father. My body never dialed to a number that made him feel proud. Felt the gravity of his anger pressed against me. Springs of innocence contorted and snapped from the heaviness of disappointment. I was a measurement of abnormality that my Father felt needed to be corrected. How easily I could weigh the thoughts of death.

My life as paper began at 1993. Felt the marks of a pulsating heart wishing it could express and make connections. Creases of the world made their way and crumbled parts of my parchment. Ripped apart whenever the words never matched my feelings or even my thoughts. My surface scribbled with imagination of a stuttering teenage boy. How he learned he could be beautiful amongst the lines; how he started to learn the ugliness that resides in him through the seeping ink.

I notice myself abyss around 2002. Descended into emotions and feelings too confusing to even have names for. Pressurized by this absence I carried. Felt the depth of my loneliness. Discovered this saturation of unresolved anger, anchoring grief, and drowning want for love; sank into my own vast darkness. My loving Mother, transformed herself ocean that year, current her arms around me, even if she did not understand. Reminded me I was still her son, that I still had reason to feel connected in this world.

2009 I share a forest with my Nanay. In the middle of the night she spoke to groves of mango trees no longer physically here. We spoke of their names, share stories of their sweetness that still lingered in our hearts. I learned to brave the darkness for her. Learn that the absence of light, did not equate to the absence of love. That I could invite courage and love in this dark forest we shared. That fear and loneliness did not have to take up so much space. This is the year I learned to be a bridge of dreams. Expanded my heart and mind to love and exist beyond this physical world. Wrote in the late nights as I witness my Nanay crossing to the other side. Eventually becoming a mango tree with the others.

2015 I made myself medicine. Would hear my mother agonizing in pain and would provide dosages of my care. Hands massaging a back aching from coughing. Her lips draining into my ears the heavy stories she wanted to tell. Offered her my face for her to touch, so we both could feel a moment of softness in this jagged world. Watched my brother Sid turn himself into medical tubes. Provided her with the vital things needed for her to keep living. Knew she was struggling yet helped ease her pain. We were all broken smiles, finding the wholeness of it all with one another.

2016 I became flowers. Wilted when I was not in season. Bloomed when everything was in play. Felt the dormancy of hope in seeds I carry. Felt ache to push beyond the shell, beyond this dark earth I buried myself beneath. Accept the warmth of those who shined on me. Graciously accepted the water those cared to share with me. This is the year my mother became a mango tree. I tore all the flowers in my chest for her. Colored her physical absence with the garden she left in me. Felt the barren soil I carried. Knew there would be more flowers again. More reason to grow, to expand, to unfurl what I have inside of me.

Petals Against My Forehead

I hoarded all these marigolds,
felt the knees, the back,
the shoulder ached carrying
these accumulations of blooms.
I kept bringing them with me
finally exhaustion took its toll.
I dropped to the ground,
muscles wept at our fatigue,
bones apologized over and over
at how we could not hold it all together.
Saw these marigolds pour out,
kissed me as if I was sacred,
took in by the soil and buried me sweetly.
Felt the dirt decay
all who I thought I needed to be,
water seeped and cradled this seed I became.
Suckled the earth with this root sprung from me.
Crawled above the ground
the sun chanted for me to keep rising.
The wind recited prayers all around me.
I marigold into existence.
Picked by the hands of children.
Placed on altars.
Collected and carried.
Kissed all the weary.

I Enter Eden

I will not come to you pure,
nor will I come to you drenched in filth and sin.
I will not return to you the same,
I may carry similarities familiar to you,
but I will be clothed in garments new to you,
woven with stories I have accumulated and experienced.

I will not arrive to you perfect,
I will not excuse what you may call flaws,
meteors of life impacted
and formed craters of dimples on me.
Fault lines of a story line
I could not keep together—split me
yet I remain intact and still whole.

I am glazed where I need to be,
do not confuse the absence of shine,
I still want to feel the rawness,
still want to offer this unadulterated
clay of self should it be wanted.

I want to remove these instances
of disconnection so that I do not miss
the opportunity to connect to you,
this universe,
these atoms yearning to come together.

I come to enter what has always been in reach,
yet many deny their access,
even myself I had derailed entry.

When I say Eden what I mean is self,
I return to the garden within me.
Seeds I have sown from joy,
from sadness, from frustrations,

and from celebrations are blooming
beneath my feet as I walk.

These petals kiss me as if I am holy,
their perfume, their scent, wafts into the air
and proclaim me holy, worthy, divine,
they wilt all the lies
that tell me I am anything less then sacred,
uplift me to walk tall
and beg me to bloom with them.

Colors of prayers wrap themselves around me,
I carry a scroll of all the ancestors who love me,
even the ones who have never touched my face
nor shared breath with me.
This same scroll scribes names of children
I will be ancestor for and will love and protect.

This bridge between here and ancestors
becomes a dreamy reality that inhales
and exhales so fluently into one another
that I am uncertain who is carrying who,
yet realizing it is I dancing with all,
singing with all who I love and who love me.

When I say Eden,
what I mean is a place of all,
even in my moments of solitude
how all refuse me to be alone and feel forgotten.

When I enter,
I am all the memories and feelings,
I am all the people and the dead,
I am me, an entirety encapsulated into singularity
in this speck of time among many.
I am an outpour of Eden,
these trails of flower behind me, in front of me,
we bloom mindfully and intentionally ahead
at the pace of my heart.

STAGNANT

penguins have left my icy cave,
warned me I was too cold.
saw me bringing in chunks of glacier
huddled amongst themselves
built an ark, gathered all the pebbles.
collected trinkets of our promises of joy,
and proceeded to leave.
wanted me to see them perform this act.
hoped I stop them, make home again,
I put blocks of frozen into the empty.
heads down they marched into their ship,
blank, bare, bleak.

Peace Be With Me

First time I learned to sleep
peacefully alone in a dark room
my Grandma had just passed
away. Before as child
I always had company,
shared floor with my bros,
shared bed with Nanay, Mom, or Dad,
floor of my brothers' room,
my own bed in shared room with bro Sid.

When I finally got a room,
did not know how to deal without
bro or anyone immediately
close by, silence too crowded with my
own thoughts, space never felt mine,
ghost of the many varieties
invited over by fears I carried,
music I played to focus away to slumber,
TV timer gave me 15, 30, 60, or 120
minutes to doze into hibernation,
some nights I would blindly
reach for remote to squeeze more
time out of that tube.

When I shared room with Grandma
I first reverted to child
felt the peace of my memories of her
taking care of me. Sleep felt
nice. Nostalgia interrupted when she
needed my assistance to get up from bed,
asked for me in middle of the night,
saw family members I physically missed.
I learned to be present for her,
learned to be more than fear for her,
learned how to love differently, intentionally.

After some months, my duties to watch
over my Grandma finally took its toll.
I was weak and weary.
Work and taking care of her drained me.
My capacity spent. I asked
Sid and my Mom for help.
I felt I failed Nanay and family.
Slept by myself with music in Sid's room.
Wish I was stronger for her.
Did not know she would pass
away less than a month later.

First time I returned to my room
I felt the guilt of not being there for her.
Did not sleep that night
thought about eulogy,
thought about Nanay,
thought about my own loneliness.
Mom and Sid next day gave me ease,
saw me not as less but someone
who loved Nanay as much as them.
Next night, I remembered my Grandma

was spirit now, did not mind if she visited.
Wind chime outside softly
dances with the breeze.
Felt her protect me again,
gave company to a silence
that use to always haunt me.
Did not play
music or leave a TV on.
I slept.

GIFT OF SELF

hides his dimple when noticed,
chubby cheeks blush,
gives in and radiates a smile.

ask questions that expose
colors of your spirit,
thanks you, especially when felt,
places hand over heart
lets you know where he stores memory.

feral laughter,
giggling buffoon,
tender chortles,
even his villainous snickers.

sharing his connection to your pain,
    truthfully reminds you that you matter,
calls you all these magnificent things
  admits he struggles to see such
        quality in himself,
lets you tell him about his brilliance
   unfolds his arms to have your words
     strike directly into his chest
       breathes, tries not to cry, fails.

rejects you apologizing habitually,
challenges you to expand

    take up fucking space and to not shrink
      wants you to be the universe you are,
claims you medicine and becomes
present to the dosage that is you,
reciprocates and prescribes his care
does not force you to take his offering,
his face lights up if you do.

imagination is uncanny
paints you with metaphors,
makes you poem
sees you, seeds you, sends you
where you need to go.

HATCHED

                    I eggshell
          at the touch   of your skin,
        felt the breaking   of a protected
      me, committed this   want for you, tore
    this membrane of hesitation,   tasted your lips,
  your tongue broke this yolk and   I forget all I am until
I felt encapsulated by you. birthing   this connection between us,
we felt bones forming from the   sound of our laughter, felt secured
  our tangled fingers ignited   feathers out our skin, we became
    understood and we found   ourselves at the death of all our
      lifetimes, found ourselves   at every birth we emerged
        out of, I found you call   the moment nothing and
          surrendered to it. maybe   forever. maybe not
            even for tomorrow.   certainty now.
              breathing the   present. inhaling
                you. exhaling   me. repeat.
                      repeat.   resound.

PI CES

frag   emo ions disper e
b rely func   yet t y ng.
t ou hts sca t red   acros
h w do   one col ect,
 ow   oes ne   r main int ct,
ho   does o fe l wh le ag in?
i si g br ken m lodie
rec te   incom let   pr y rs
h pe t me wil f ll t e res .

STATIC

What happens when you
no longer trust your memory?
when your memory
no longer trusts you?

What happens when your memory
refuses to be vivid?
removing all colors
because you keep replaying
the memory.

What happens when your memory
removes all the shapes and lines?
refuses to be clear,
becomes simply blurry
    every time you retrieve it.

What happens when your memory leaves you?
asks you to quit following for them.

What happens when a memory
takes the soft part of your heart? tells you to remain
    while they go.

What happens when your memory
claims you unsacred?
calls you too broken of a temple.

What happens when your memory becomes distance?
manifests into a place
    you can no longer reach.

What happens when your memory
begs you to quit remembering?
knows you are hurting yet goes.

You stay and pray,
even if the prayers feel broken
you pray anyway.
You be still and sing,
voice chants
    eventually cracks, splits faultline,
        turns you into a valley, a canyon.
You let go trying to find memory,
instead find a self waiting for you,
and you move on.
You breathe and offer peace to yourself.
You breathe and be peace for yourself.
You move forth.
You stumble,
get up and move forth.
You be kind to yourself.
You invite kindness and be present when it is offered.

Memory finds reasons to return to you,
brings a heart you thought you lost. You continue to move.
You go, keep going. You love, you always love.

Portal

Let me be flood, more than this controlled reservoir of water. Let me be tidal wave, I do not care to be a sea of calm. Let me be a storm of violent water descending down, break me away from being a gentle puffy nimbus.

Yet I find myself hesitant to be anything than barren. Is there grief without the outpour of saline? Why must I offer water and salt drawn from a well that is close to empty?

I do not know where this mango tree is suppose to grow, what side of the bridge of dreams was this mango tree suppose to take root. Why am I more planet than human, more floating orb than an entity with ancestors?

My tribes of both sides of this bridge, why am I given this mango tree to grow when I can barely water myself.

How many passes around the sun do I have to make to move on?

This mango tree could only thrive in this realm that is me.

This concrete jungle we call physical, sun and water nourishingly plentiful but soil and air lacks stories and prayers its roots and leaves long for.

This mystic dream we call heaven, vibrant air and soil in abundance but water and moonlight are not meant to flourish mangos yearning to burst from its branches.

I forget my sacredness and that I am orb and bridge, a portal of worlds. That my well is offerings from ancestors and I only need to ask should I feel empty and they will provide until I am an outpour of their love which is always accessible to me if I am open. This tree, resembling this grief that may never seem to leave me, is hugged and cared for by tribes of family and friends in this physical world who intentionally choose to never leave me uncared for unless I foolishly give them reason to.

My loves, take all the sea water in this ocean in me until you feel I have wept enough.

Ugly Heart

I have an ugly heart,
kind left alone because of noticeable bruises,
kind one leaves on the tree, falls on its own, rots and decomposes,
kind that gets too much sun,
kind that does not get enough sun,
kind that is home to worms,
kind that does not ship well,
kind that is perishable and decays quickly,
kind that never gets tasted, fear that its flavor matches its look,
kind that obviously cross pollinated, mutated, became unrecognizable,
kind that gets hard to talk about,
kind that is weird and unlike anything,
kind that is sweet when ripe,
kind that is unapologetically bitter,
kind that is taken as medicine,
kind that is poison,
kind that hurts ugly,
kind that uglys tenderly, softly, kindly,
kind that blooms forgiveness,
kind that sees the world as magnificent,
kind that is worth a peel,
kind that laughs,
kind that cries,
kind that writes poems,
kind that remembers,
kind that sings, sings loudly, sings ugly,
kind that quits trying to be beautiful,
kind that abandons being handsome,
kind that I call my own,
kind that calls me its own even when I abandoned it,
kind that is still heart,
kind that is always heart,
kind that ugly feels seen,
kind that ugly knows it is loved.

SAPWOOD

eaten a thousand worms
hoping they break down
butterflies that never migrated
out of my stomach.
they only found dead poems
I was too coward to write.
ate rotten parchment
freed moths slumbering beneath
escaped the cave of my mouth
while I was sleeping.
extracted juice from the decaying fruit
dropped from a tree
growing out of my chest.
found the axe in my hand
wounds on the trunk
attempts to chop it away.
whispered that I not remove
richness of my nectar
carried away the hatchet from my grip.

Inheritance

My mom told me how when she was young in the Philippines
My father would come over when my grandfather was working overseas
He would check on my Nanay and the rest of my family.
My mom told me how even at a young age
My father would playfully say he would marry her one day
In context, my mother was set to devoting her life to God,
As a young teenager, she had complications
Which led her to believe she would not have children one day.
This was okay because this gave her more reason to become a nun.
She dated, but no one caught her eye.
My father would even be out of the picture
When he enlisted in the United States Coast Guard.
It wouldn't be until my uncle, my father's brother
Was severely sick and everyone believed he would not make it.
My father returned back to visit my uncle.
This would be the moment my father caught sight of my mom again.
This is when my mom wanted to be with my dad more than
    becoming a nun.
They would soon marry and move to the United States.

I have inherited my hatred from my father.
As a child I was his tabachoy
whom he would affectionately pinch
the side of my gut whenever I passed him.
When I was nine years old
my father gave up his Coast Guard life
for the sake of my mother's sanity
and to help raise his three sons.
I didn't know what to expect from his homecoming.
Only understood I should respect him
for his sacrifice to provide for this family
and that he has a temper
which boiled and spilled over
on me or whomever he was angry at
After awhile my father became tired of how I looked

would grab the side of my gut
and with my flesh in his hand say to me
"Damn it tabachoy.
This is like Michelin tire.
This is ugly. You need to lose this."
Then he would scrutinize what I ate
scolded me till every bite I took tasted like shame.
I soon learned how it felt to be empty.
How deep of an abyss my shame could create.
I could never eat enough food to feel full.

I have inherited my mother's loving spirit.
To my mother, I was her baby.
When I got older her Baby Lakay
which translated to baby adult.
As her Baby Lakay she didn't mind that I was fat.
She would pull me aside now and then
to tell me to be mindful of my weight
not because of how I looked
but because she was concerned about my health
To her, I was always guapo no matter what.
"Ala, my Baby Lakay is growing up so quick.
Pretty soon you won't be a Baby no more anak.
I love you my Baby Lakay."
Though my stomach always struggled to feel full,
it was because of my mother
I understood how full a heart could feel.

My father's Ilokano temper
would melt the core of his heart
pumping hot magma through his veins.
I felt his infliction of fear brand
itself against my ass when his aim was on.
His belt, a nearby stick, or even his hand
didn't hold back his frustrations,
his disappointments, his anger.
There was no discussion of his actions,
only an understanding that he was my dad,
which needed no more explaining than that.

"Damn shit, why you always talking back huh?
Come here! You think I'm dumb?
Why you quiet now huh? Ukinam!
Quit crying or I'll pak pak your puet again."

My mother spanked and pinched
with an intent to put me and my brothers
in line and in check.
Her loving spirit and caring nature
always made it hard for her to discipline
us through an act of violence,
which is why she always followed
through with words of love and understanding.
"Anak, come here.
You got to be good okay?
Don't be causing foolishness all the time anak.
I know you sometimes are hard-headed
and get real angry like your dad
but you got to try to do better. Okay?
Please, for me anak."

My father was the first person
to teach me how to hate my body
"If you are fat, no one will love you."
These words would be repeated
through the voice of a doctor,
"You can't date if you're fat"
aunties and family members would say,
"Anak, no one will date you if you're tabachoy"
my own fucking lips,
"I don't deserve to be loved."

Judgment, my father never strays
from making me understand his place.
He takes it upon himself to voice
opinions I never asked for nor wanted.
I can never have a conversation with him
because they always manifest into arguments
which I never win because I love him

more than he loves me;
I listen with my heart and mind open
while he briefly hears my words
to check how I am wrong by all means.
He is not afraid to hate me.

When I was 23, I looked at my mother
and told her I was depressed.
She didn't know what to say to me.
But she knew what to do at the moment
… hug me.
I'm pretty sure her heart was broken
that she didn't know how to help me.
but it didn't stop her from being there for me
didn't stop her from loving me.

Love, my mother never had to find a reason to love me.
She just did.
She bravely tells me stories
offers me the tales of her pain
the struggles of her trials and tribulations.
I open my ears to her the way she has opened her heart to me.
She is a constant reminder
that I always have a heart to call home.
I have learned to build a home out of my own heart
because of her.

AS WE LONG

my sis Arlene brings a deer tonight
and I will make space for it
who is to say this deer is not ancestor
there is a deer in this poem
what I mean to say is there is a deer in here
I will bring my nose to hers
we all will bring our noses to hers
we share breath as we always have
we all breathe
and proclaim one another's existence
because how can we not celebrate
this life before us
this life in us
there is a deer in this room
I will whisper to her
names of all I miss in this physical plane
let us all whisper names to her
there are now herds of deer in this room
they found the salt to lick in all our chests
from dried tears we all have wept through the years
they found joy in being remembered
they found reason to prance right now in this poem
inside this room.
my sis Arlene brought a deer into this room
and it appears everyone else has too.
I want to recite all the words I know
so that this poem can go forever
so that all these deer remain in here longer
but their journeys, all our journeys
are not limited to this poem, this room.
we all know this so we kiss
these deer in this room, in front of us,
bless this poem bringing deer into this room
bless these deer finding room in us
even when this poem ends.

COMMUNE WITH SALT AND WATER

there is a bitter joy
in not grieving alone.
how the body can fully collapse
release the feeling of whole
surrender the body of water we are
into these crevices and faultlines
speaking of an overwhelming absence.
falling into each other like praying
hands trying to grasp life claimed by death
how our faces frown honesty
that we are not okay,
that mourning is excruciating,
that remaining hurts and part of us is dead.
grief is not joyous.
grief exists because we have loved
the heart continues to love
and we are an outpour of mess
a flood having no where to go.

CEMENTED DREAM

seeing a father and son dance todo
todo, I want the reel to reply
continuously, let this be prayer,
make their tenderness a proclamation,
rejoice in their smiles and claim
heaven on a concrete driveway
made into a dance floor today,
break all the bread serve all the rice
share all the tortillas naan flatbread
until we are fed and nourished by this moment,
manifest this gospel lost amongst
violence of men, shed wars
we carried too long in these congested
chests we armor with pride with hurt
with illusions we think our hearts
need to project to sustain a way of dying,
bless this son and father making
softness exist among all the hardness
constantly constraining us,
freedom that can belong to all
living in a joy that feels as if it should
collapse from its own weight but how
love would not let that happen.

EXCAVATED EXCLAMATION

pray the earth before digging.
enter the ground as a visitor.
remove the dirt, the clay,
the piles of rocks. unfold
layers of lifetimes
compressed into ashes,
debris, and sentiments. do not
dismiss what is in front as you dig
deeper and unravel more. drink water,
pause the excitement of discovery,
and tend the present self.
snack a joy as you take a deep breath.
return to task. understand when to abandon
shovel and dedicate the process to brushes.
fingers work their way through pebbles and soil.
touch of calcium is made.
reveal more so the sky and sun can see as well.
hands touch skeleton remains of what
appears to be hips, femur, claws. eyes
gasp at the sight of ribs, of spine, of horns.
fossilized head appears and you proclaim
ancestor even though science will say
you have no DNA relations. you remind
science they miss the true
connection in their statement, as if family
can only be told through blood. forgetting
we are all stardust, carbon, and all between.
you sing songs because the dead never
die unless we stop remembering. you
bring ancient back into the today.
you call this ritual joyous. press your nose
against the hollow remain of theirs
and breathe deeply to share
breath. inhale a story unknown.
exhale your journey to them.

Sexy Be

Sexy does not always mean to evoke
the sultry but if the breeze calls for it,
lure what gravitates to have
dialogue with your skin and
cut what does not know how to hold
a conversation of attraction.
Sexy not always a furnace of heat
but if the sun dances for your flame,
ignite a radiance worth
traveling the speed of light for, and should
someone with cold intentions try to encapsulate
your shine, be amber of a thousand aunties,
torch what does not know how to hold you.
Sexy has no need to conjure the interest of eyes
but should the pupils of pineapples affirm
you are worthy of stares, let your flesh
sing the hymns that makes
all the feathers from a flock of peacocks
sway to your heartbeat, and should a spectator
seek you without knowing how to gaze
without hunger, siren them against rocky
shores that will devour without hesitation.
Sexy through intelligence, imagining
dimensions and opening portals that drive
neurons into radical bliss, electrifying
spines with an articulation of liberation.
Sexy gangster as fuck, gives thyself
permission to exist without external validation,
stands with an autonomy that does not fear
one's own fierceness nor sways
away to the delicacy of tenderness,
a walking balisong in perpetual
state of grace and sharpness.
Sexy in breath, compressing
and decompressing the flow of air,

bellows the body into a meditative
trance of a here all wish to approach
and enter, lungs whirlwind a lifetime
upon each inhale and exhale.
Sexy because.
Sexy tangible.
Sexy the spell of loving the self always.

Flourish

I want to run my fingers
through the plumerias
growing from her spine.
Lean my head on the pool
of lilies on her collar,
take in the coolness
she brings into my life.
Caress the roses growing
wildly from her neck, gently
kiss the thorns that protect her.
Comb my hands
through the field of sunflowers in her hair,
massage the earth beneath her follicles of stems,
hope to give all the tension in her head
reason to move on. I surrender to the tulips
on her face, feel the petals touch mine,
she awoke all the seasons asleep in me.
Stared at her pupil of peonies,
watch them dilate and unfurl before me,
confess I cannot take my eyes away from her.
I revealed to her the lotus in my chest,
told how it blooms more each time I am with her.
I know she is a garden that does not need
my tending, but I am here to witness
and be enamored by all she is.
She is all the flower I long for.

Scaled Lifetime

Is this the lifetime where we were part of the reptilian race living on a planet with 6 moons (4 broken from needless space wars) and 3 suns that we keep slipping into orbit of each one that we forget which galaxy we reside in? The one where we lost all our children to a plague. One where we almost lost each other because we wanted to be consumed with grief more than each other. One where we bit each other's tails off consensually calling it foreplay that led us to this blissful euphoria of pain and pleasure. One where we pretended to be the elite only to take down its bougie regiment. One where I went blind at one point, but woke up each morning pretending to look at your face, truthfully called you gorgeous and stunning. One where you laugh and I peed involuntarily from the joy of hearing it. One where… oh this is not that lifetime. My bad.

ASHES

someday you learn to be the forest
when all had been burned. take
inventory of what is lost, and what
remains. still feel bits of ember
scattered through you
and it is difficult to get past being
devastated from it all.
quit briefly trying to repair while all
is still smoldering and unsafe.
submit, become grief. collapse,
implode into one's self, and crumbled
into a state of ashes. how can you even learn
to hope again? yet you omit that ending
is even on option. spores of mushrooms
decay these hurt parts of ourselves.
fungus breaking down this state of confusion
and pray you into an emergence.
sun kisses you still.
believes in your resiliency,
reminds you have always been timeless
and that this is a speck to the infinity you are.
feel the trees in you not claimed or still standing,
dare branch out to flesh this landscape of you again.
seeds in you sprout, adorn your earthly
body with green leaves and ferns.
flowers burst out your chest.
bees, birds, bears, and all other woodland creatures
return and call you habitable again.
you bathe under the rain,
water touches you sacred,
eons of lifetimes awaken to be again in you.
you always a forest.

To Heal

I do not put our conversations under autopsy. what clue could I possibly find that would make her feel differently about me? bless the indifference that takes over automatically, knew the earth—an element so connected with all—would tremble trying to retrieve me. body limps itself numbs my mind and coats a protective membrane around my heart called loneliness. how easily we forget this slug of an emotion understands us so deeply because it is a composite of hopes that could not love us back. I no longer look at this creature as hideous but a ghost child reaping in these desires which I sometimes am too stubborn or afraid to lay to rest. magnificent being, does not suffocate or overstay their welcome since I have chosen to be more gentle and attentive to what they have to say. even learned to howl for solitude to take over and become the ritual when all is felt with honesty. feel this carabao of my entity call the roosters and hens of my ancestors to carry me unto the back of this horned hooved animal. hear in the dark all of them crowing and clucking to me prayers to my travel. exhausted and weary I barely can hold to stay on, felt the branches of mango trees making sure I do not fall, did not care the irritation it left on my skin, I remembered briefly and called them Mom and Nanay. They left me fruits, I cried to stay but they kissed me anak, and I knew this was not my place yet. finally I arrive at my bahay, my body. place my nose against the carabao's own, we breathe together until all that was left is me. I sing psalms for all that holds me, remains to connect with me, that love with infinity.

OPTIC

I have been talking to the sun,
because the moon knows
too many of my secrets. I do not
mind that the sun is a bad listener.
I care not for my words to be remembered
by the sun, there is a relief that my confessions
will simply evaporate under all those rays.
sun really believes in new days.
unlike the night, who retains all within the grim.
darkness always feels old and pressed
against my marrow. sun does not ask
me questions and I am okay with this.
in fairness, I only talk to the sun to hear myself.
I articulate a dim that the sun can barely understand.
I shook my fist to the sky and the sun
barely gave a shit, if any. but my shadow
hears everything. does not snitch me
out to either, instead holds me with patience,
even when the body heated with rage,
even when the heart goes cold,
even when I think I am forgotten.

I'VE BEEN STARING AT BATTLEGROUNDS WITHIN ME,

it is the young warrior burning in me
eagerly wanting to go into the fields
not caring if he is unprepared or unequipped to combat
ready to test himself until his spirit
is victorious or exhausted in defeat

it is the datu developing in me
who takes a moment
presses his nose against others ungngo the people around him
looks at the home he has built and shared
reminding himself of why he must defend
builds a strategy
because he seeks to win the war not just the battles

it is the babaylan awakening in me
that understands there will be wounds to mend
offers stories to the village within me so that hope is never lost
prescribes one to drink, eat, sing, laugh or dance
giving reasons to always celebrate and live

it is the farmer growing in me
ready to tend the destruction and casualties
breathing the landscape within.
    longing to be plowed and planted
learning patience is just as important as water
grounding himself with
the roots of the values he has sowed

it is the prayer in me
knowing I am an answer to the struggles in me
who loves despite the world telling him he cannot
who is thankful for the past but pushes to move forward
surrenders to the presence of peace so he may always have the
courage to fight

How To Seduce a Tornado

watch them flex
   their puffy clouds.
whisper warmly into their ear
    watch them melt at your every word.
pretend not to hear their rumble.
giggle at the hail they try to toss at you.
look away and call them silly,   foolish.
be so much earth they pain
 how inaccessible you can become
   they lust at this magnetic
 force you are.
remind them you can love yourself better.
humble every entitlement they
  think they can have with you,
    because you owe no one you.
watch them funnel to be greater.
  shout to let them know they are seen.
    watch them whirl, passion swirling rapidly.
     pull their face,
   share breath,
  lock eyes,
   kiss.
confess you want them.
feel all that cannot be held down
be swept and taken.
lose track whose
  limbs are whose.
liberate in collective destruction,
 travel until this intimacy
  becomes simply a wind
    pushing a tumbleweed
     across the other's chest.
exhaust.
exhale.
exclaim.

WHEN YOU WERE CATERPILLAR

devouring your way across the garden
I thought you would consume me
crawling against my stem
only to feel you cocoon
beneath some of my leaves.
wind's songs sounded sweeter,
sun's warmth felt glorious on my leaves,
even night skies spoke stories
I never witnessed until your presence.
your company helped me feel I existed.
emerged out your threads a stranger.
butterflied where I could not go
had no language to tell you to return
only opened the secret of my bloom
you drew the nectar of my letter
felt the softness of your wings
against the lush of my petals.
knew this was not the lifetime
yet still we had this,
maybe the next one.

Whale Poop

Excrete plumes near surface.
Fecal feathers out of you,
flocks migrate from warm body to cold ocean.
Cloud once clear waters,
disturb the sea with your bowels,
hatch the circle of life so easily forgotten.
Often ignored how much richness
resides in the murkiness.
clarity does not always feed,
phytoplanktons pleased by the poo.
Do not constrain the goodness majestic creature.
Exaltation flush out of you.
Gaggle a smirk at the thought,
mustering the realization that you are the shit.

Recollection of None

Mom,
I do not remember my last words with you.
Pretty sure my brother Sid and I were leaving
your hospital room and it was a routine I love you,
kind of routine where you know it might be the last.
I do not remember our last conversation.
Was I supposed to remember, Mom?

BODY OF WATER

wind chimes outside my window play.
I say hi to my Nanay and Mom.
think they know I want to cry
know they are not the reason,
I hear them anak me,
I can only deeply breathe
though I am afraid to drown.
they remind me I am 90% tears
most which are more joyous
than this sorrow I think I am.
"Anak, be glad you water,
though you do not hold shape
like the earth you are loving
enough to let yourself be held by soil,
while wind is so free and graceful
you brave to evaporate into the air
form clouds of understanding
become this symphony of rain for all,
you do not ignite passionately like fire
yet you will sing with flames
into a soup or tea giving a melody
of warmth that can be felt deep within."
wind chimes settled and I miss them.

THRIVE

What will they do to your art
when it is no longer sweet
no longer easy for them to digest
no longer consumable for the masses?

Tell me what happens to your art
when it is labeled unsuccessful,
will you take on the role as failure?

When they claim your art,
take away the shapes
you composed from wrinkles of your ancestors,
take away the colors
you mixed to match the cheeks of your children,
take away its meaning
you drew from your own heart,
how much of you will be left?

We have been told
that our stories do not belong to us.
How we witness textbooks
make liars out of grandparents.
How we listen to lectures
illustrating how our parents are undeveloped.
How we lived through an education
teaching us why we should hate ourselves.

Who are we surviving for?
Will our art thrive past survival?
Can we imagine ourselves past survival?

We are not strangers
who accidentally stumbled upon art.
We are vessels of stories
who burst the moment our spirits touched canvas.

We brushed strokes of our struggles.
Photographed the landscapes of our conditions.
Written testimonies of our triumphs

We had always been successful,
how our truth is our currency towards freedom,
our imagination is the wealth the future will inherit,
our love is the richness that shapes this world.

Survival is never the end of our stories.
Our art is us surviving and so much more.
We are creators, we are destroyers,
we are culture, we are brave,
we are thriving
we are art always thriving.

TONIGHT I AM A GALAXY OF STARS

your heart a balangay
   drifting in your body of ocean
my thousand mga bituin you map
   navigate all my dim and brilliance
my darkness feels more found
than this clutter cluster of lost
your waters a power of movement
even through its stillness

vastness between us
   dissipates

Extinguish

There is a forest on fire
But maybe there is no fire
Untelevised disaster might simply be
only fabricated imagination

There is a forest on fire
But it is easier to believe that is elsewhere.
That it is happening out of our reach
What good is it for us to think of it

There is a forest on fire
But we are breathing just fine
We cannot feel the flame,
everything must be okay
It is not our problem.
It always seems to never be our problem

There is a forest on fire
But it hurts, it burns, it engulfs us to care
A forest is on fire,
our forest is on fire,
we are on fire,
burning in agony,
burning for others to notice that we are on fire,
extinguish this damn fire.

INGRESS

I portaled.
did not check if I was ready to be received.
I set my coordinates. looked
over the calibration of this transporter
in my chest to see if it was suited to transmit
this entity of me to the location of my attraction,
person whom all my skipped
heartbeats escaped to, face that magnificently
disrupted my bubble of normalcy enough for me to dare
stretch time and space to explore these feelings.
not all timelines are meant to be jumped.
not all space is compatible to welcome me.
getting caught in a frequency not meant for me.
static.
tracking lines and vibration but no analog
sense to make clarity. electric feels
mush into electrons of ectoplasma.
ghost.
lingering wave caught in a loop.
cycle.
lost without gravity to pull back,
or even without a current to push a direction.
boop. boop. beep.

APRICITY

despite the cold, you still offer
yourself to me. I do not bring to notice
seeing you less, instead celebrate each
kiss of your warmth when we meet.
I appreciate the invitation when you
remind me of you, stretching from this window
trying to touch my skin, tenderly giving
me an excuse to sneak away to you. chill
seeps into my bones as I peel myself
away from the comforts of home to experience you.
I surrender. let my face and all my exposed
exterior belong to you for that moment.
bursting through my ribs—violets, chrysanthemums,
solidago, cyclamen, sweet asylum—overwhelmed
from your embrace. in your presence I
relearn the value of radiance,
relearn how to receive when all feels barren.

WHEN ASKED WHAT MY FAVORITE COLOR IS

I would say your name

confess how I wake up
aching for a taste of your hue

I am saturated with your kindness
dyed with the stains of your stories
my smile tinges a glow because of you

pigmentations of you
graffiti themselves all over my dream

my thoughts enameled
with the different shades of you
I am tattooed with the chroma of your being

you refract the light I radiate
give it a value that tints the truths about me

paint yourself against me

you color me

color me

In a dark room I am eating

pan de ube. Delicious. It will
probably soak the Jameson
drank from earlier. I do not care;
only occupied with chewing
morsels of purple suspended
amongst the baked grains.
I write this in hopes
spirits will not wake
me up to scribble an early
morning poem. The poems
can be too honest at those times.
I am too poor for truth,
too broken to want more.
I am afraid I know what will be said.

PILLOW OUR FACES AGAINST

each other, fluff these feathers
weary from flights of survival,
offer the vanes of our quills
rest in this softness, take
nest on the other's shoulders,
molt away the jaded world
hatch affection we been
incubating to share,
sing secrets that only
belong to us as if anyone
could decipher our songs.

Held

In a women's lit class,
there was an essay
where a lady talks about hugging.
How she grew
accustomed to side-hugs.
How she felt she was an awkward
person to hug because of her body.
I felt less alone that day.

I am perplexed the way young children
know how to hug me so properly.
They do not forget I am big,
yet they hug me in a way that makes
me feel I fit correctly into their world.

I did not grow up in a hugging family.
We hugged, not to the extent
where it was a daily occurrence.
As children, I am sure we hugged
all of the relatives during parties,
told to kiss and hug
this auntie and that auntie,
this lola, and that lola.
I do not remember hugging
uncles or lolos.
Maybe we did.
Or maybe it was awkward
for them to hug nephews or grandsons
who were not immediate family.

When my Father would come
home from the Coast Guard,
I remember hugging him at airports.
Even kissed his cheek on returns.
When he dropped me off to school

I would always kiss him goodbye
until one day I left without kissing him,
grew to where this ritual between a son
and a father felt embarrassing.

My Mother hugged my brothers and I.
Hugged me after I was disciplined,
brought me in closer to help me
understand why I received the pain I did.

I learned how the body can produce oxytocin
when you hold a person long enough.
Told friends I wanted to hug them longer
counted the seconds until our bodies
released this trust we always had,
solidified with this feeling of being held.

I held my Mother's hand
until she could barely keep her eyes open.
Watch her sleep away
when all I want is to be held by her once more.

I jokingly hugged my Father,
squeezed him trying to make him feel uncomfortable
until I felt him hug me and the joke dissolved,
became forgiveness and acceptance,
even if it did not feel permanent
it felt worth having, we held,
did not have an agenda of breaking any cycle
but we broke enough to have this moment.

IMPLOSION

"behind you somehow is time"
—Steve Fujimura

behind me is space
intersecting is us
pulling all the lost atoms
extracting out what lingered
   long enough
we become these pockets of dust
   of gas
collapsing all that is fragile in us
frame of calcium
  fortifying at the sight of each other
rotating the matter in our chest
universe forms where
  only a vastness of emptiness
    once resided
we are not a destination
   this is not an endpoint
simply a commitment of growth
a disturbance of found

I once was only thought,

mere speck in what seems distant future.

I once was last hope to be a girl,
round type of belly said otherwise,
still she prayed
simply that I be born into existence,

I once was child holding onto legs,
hugging thighs for a feeling of safe,
felt the nudge of palm against my back
pushing me towards sandy playgrounds,
sailing me away to those I call family,
let go into discovering beyond myself.

I once was teenager,
shouting at the softness of her heart,
my inherited anger displaced on her,
understood me while I misunderstood her,
worked to keep me kind and tender,
knew I felt all the world and hurt,
did not let me become only pain.

I once was adult,
watching parts of my heart deteriorate and leave,
grandpa whose name became mine,
nanay who watched over me,
uncle who used to always offer a smile,
cousin who was very well my brother,
mother who was why I have this heart.

I once thought I had to finish every poem,

Dear Sadness,

You visited me this morning. I have been scrolling to hopefully get rid of you. Failed. I tried to avoid listening to sad songs and although I have dodged these tunes, I feel I invited Shame and Loneliness. I am afraid to lean into all of you. That I am uncertain what healthy boundaries look like with all of us. I let go of my reluctance and kissed you all on the forehead. Claim you all sacred lessons instead of haunting spirits. Feel this knot in my stomach I woke up to, unfurl itself as I affectionately touch you all with tenderness. Grace visited us, felt their arms wrapped around me, Grace took on the image of my Nanay and Mom and I lost reasons to contain myself. Felt my Manong Richie, Grandpa, and Uncle Boy release this tension on my neck with their hands. I tell all I miss them, felt them all kiss my forehead and I wanted to fight this feeling of sacredness yet they held my face until I submitted to their truth. Felt the friends I lost become friends finding themselves in me. Loneliness hugged them all until I was the only one left to hug, only to find myself in the body of Loneliness embracing these people whom I love. Ground collected these seeds falling out of all of us. Sadness let go of my hand, carried Shame and dissolved into the earth. Flowers kissed my feet, tickled my legs, invited me to dance until I remembered all I tried to forget, sang until I felt what needed to be felt, breathed until I was only air and wind. Po the mountain, po the ocean, po the sky, po the moon and sun. Surrendered until I was all the universe, until I was nothing in its fullness.

Sincerely,
A Vessel

Notes

I.	The following were previously published works in the literary magazine, *sPARKLE & bLINK 115*, by the publishing company, Quiet Lightning. Much thanks for welcoming my works.

"Offspring of Victor Frankenstein"
"Petals Against My Forehead"
"Whale Poop"

II.	The following are ekphrastic poems.

"I Enter Eden" is an ekphrastic poem to Wanxin Zhang's sculpture, "Return to the Garden of Eden."

"Portal" is an ekphrastic poem to Kelly Akashi's sculpture "Weep."

III.	The poems, "I Enter Eden" and "Portal" were originally published in the *Claiming Space* zine printed by the arts organization, Montalvo Arts Center for the 2022 event, Refiguring the Body in Landscape.

Acknowledgements

Much thanks to the following:

To Sampaguita Press, especially my editors Keana Aguila Labra and Kelly Ritter, for doing valuable work for the community as well as building a wonderful literary community with the network you help foster. I am thankful to be part of your literary family which deeply enriches my life.

To my manongs Isidoro Mazon Dumuk, Roland Mazon Dumuk, and Robertino Ragazza, for inspiring the creative direction of the book cover. I appreciate your support not only with this book but with all my endeavors and projects.

To my brother Anthony Santa Ana, thank you for the rides to open mics across the Bay Area when we were young and I barely knew what spoken word was. You let me travel with you, and I am grateful for all the steps I have taken with you.

To my manang Arlene Biala, your support constantly dissolves my self-doubts and continues to help me grow.

To my sibling, Keana Aguila Labra, one of my favorite Virgos who helped me tremendously with the fruition of this book as well as colored my life with a much needed vibrancy. Witnessing you tackle on things and thrive helps challenge me to do the same.

To Poetry Center San Jose, I am blessed to be part of your literary community and I am grateful for all the opportunities you have given me through the years.

To all those in my life whom I affectionately call family or friend, this book exist because of your love for me. May you find yourself in one or many of these poems. I know I found parts of myself with my relationship with you.

To my Filipino Community in Silcon Valley, especially FANHS (Filipino American National Historical Society), FYC (Filipino Youth Coalition), and LEAD Filipino. These organizations make me proud of my Filipino heritage and history because of their consistent engagement with the community.

To my MALI (Multicultural Arts Leadership Institute) family, especially founder, Tamara Mozahuani Alvarado, the network's push to ensure that artists of color are sitting at the tables that help shape the infrastructure and decisions in the South Bay.

To my brothers at Ating Angkan, thank you for affirming my existence as well as providing a space to help me grow into becoming a better Filipino man.

Publisher's Note

The Philippine phrases found throughout the collection are translated into English in the following Translation Index.

We translate these phrases into English for inclusivity purposes in respect to our non-Philippine-language speaking readers, particularly BIPOC and diaspora Filipinxao readers. We also translate these phrases in order to adhere to the requirements set by some book distributors.

We are aware of the compromise we make in order to make this art more accessible to a wider audience. In translating these phrases, we participate in a global market that continues to be dictated by Western- and English-supremacist practices. We are also aware that these simple, direct translations of words fall short in communicating their cultural weight and meaning.

We acknowledge the history of translating devices used violently as tools of white gaze revisionism, for the cultural erasure and othering of non-Western, Global South, and diaspora art. This includes the related practice in the United States publishing industry of italicizing words from non-English languages. Our current policy is not to italicize these words.

As cultural discourse, translation methods, and language resources evolve with the times, so may our formatting and translating practices at Sampaguita Press. It is our dream and goal to be able to have our titles commercially available and translated into different languages other than English, for greater language and literary equity.

Translation Index

The page numbers follow the print edition of HELD. Words may appear multiple times throughout the book. Here we list their first appearance.

Because the author is Ilocano, we have denoted the language as Ilocano. However, we understand words share meaning across the 177+ Philippine languages, and acknowledge this kapamilya of Philippine languages even though we cannot name them all.

Vanga: (15) A Filipino ceramic vase used to store fish for fermentation
Bagoong: (15) A Filipino condiment made from salted and fermented seafood
Nanang; (15) Ilocano for Mom
Nanay: (15) An endearing name for grandma
Bulilit: (15) A small type of mackerel
Asin: (15) Ilocano for salt
Maysa:(25) Ilocano for 1
Dua: (25) Ilocano for 2
Tallo: (25) Ilocano for 3
Uppat: (25) Ilocano for 4
Lima: (25) Ilocano for 5
Innem: (25) Ilocano for 6
Pito: (25) Ilocano for 7
Walo: (25) Ilocano for 8
Tabachoy: (51) A nickname for someone who is fat or chubby
Anak: (52) Children, often said with affection
Ala: (52) Oh my goodness
Lakay: (52) Ilocano for adult
Ukinam: (53) Ilocano for fuck
Pak pak: (53) Spank
Puet: (53) Ilocano for butt.
Todo todo: (57) A type of cha cha that is usually danced to the song, "Todo, Todo," by Daniela Romo
Carabao: (64) Ilocano for water buffalo

Bahay: (64) Ilocano for home
Datu: (66) Ilocano for chief
Ungngo: (66) A Filipino greeting similar to Polynesian's, hongi, where one presses one's nose with another, and share breath to honor one another along with the ancestors
Babaylan: (66) A Filipino priestess or shaman
Balangay: (74) A whale
Mga bituin: (74) Stars
Po: (85) Shorten version of mano po, which is a gesture reserved for elders or those older than you. One would take an elder's hand and press their own forehead against the back of the elder's hand

About the Author

Lorenz Mazon Dumuk (he/they) has two chapbook collections of poetry, *Ay Nako: Writing Through the Struggle*, and *I Think In Poetry*. He is an alumnus of VONA and MALI (Multicultural Arts Leadership Institute), a Silicon Valley based program that focuses on developing leaders of color in the arts, culture, and entertainment sectors. He is one of the curators for Glowing with the Moon, an open mic and interactive community space in San Jose.

Lorenz writes with, against, and through the contradictions he encounters, which allows him to explore the different silences in his life through his poetry. He's an awkwardly adorable poet who can be caught doing hip-circles before a poetry reading.

Land Acknowledgement

This book was written on Ojibwe, Odawa and Potawatomi lands and produced on Ohlone and Tongva lands.

The staff at Sampaguita Press acknowledge we are settlers on the stolen sacred lands of these Peoples. We remember their connection to these regions and give thanks for the opportunity to live, teach, and learn in their traditional homelands. May we create connections with them, and may we learn Indigenous protocols to become honorable stewards of the land.

We encourage you, Reader, to:

- Amplify the voices of Indigenous people leading grassroots change movements
- Donate your time and money to Indigenous-led organizations
- Politically support the Land Back Movement

In line with these encouragements, Sampaguita Press supports Indigenous art and donates a portion of Press funds raised to Indigenous-led organizations.

In reflecting on our own lives and remembering our family histories, we must remember the legacies of colonialism that we have benefitted from and continue to benefit from as settler-colonialists.

From Palestine to the Philippines, none of us are free until all of us are free.

About Sampaguita Press

Sampaguita Press is an independent micropress publishing house based in San Jose, California. We publish works by and for artists of color. We acknowledge the intersections of identity and support the LGBTQIA+ folk/x in communities of color as well.

Sampaguita Press was founded in 2021 by poets and creatives who wanted to create a space and platform for ourselves, our peers, and other fellow voices who are underrepresented in mainstream publishing.

We strive to inspire progressive change. We acknowledge that change is made with solidarity. We honor and nurture the relationships between our fellow communities. We especially seek works that broaden perspectives and foster understanding.

We believe in racial and social equity. We acknowledge that Western literature and publishing are still overwhelmingly white spaces, and we are committed to amplifying underrepresented voices by providing attention and care to artists who may not have access to traditional publishing spaces.

We are an intersectionally feminist & womanist, inclusive press. We prioritize artists of color of all genders. We discourage hegemonic narratives; hierarchical structures; and supremacist, assimilationist, and normative messaging.

We are a safe literary & linguistic space, and we welcome chapbook submissions in non-English languages.

We support Indigenous rights and sovereignty over the land known as the United States. Our support goes out to the Indigenous groups everywhere in the world who have been harmed, silenced, and displaced. We encourage our readers to learn about and support Indigenous Peoples.

Printed in the USA
CPSIA information can be obtained
at www.ICGtesting.com
LVHW040826271124
797656LV00009B/1046